E. ALLISON PEERS PUBL
LECTURES 4

Pilgrimages to St James of Compostella from the British Isles during the Middle Ages

Robert Brian Tate

LIVERPOOL UNIVERSITY PRESS

This lecture was delivered on 20 November 1989 in the Senate House of the University of Liverpool

First published 1990 by
LIVERPOOL UNIVERSITY PRESS
PO Box 147
Liverpool L69 3BX

Copyright © Robert Brian Tate

All rights reserved. No part of this publication may be reproduced, stored in a retrieval system, or transmitted, in any form, or by any means, electronic, mechanical, photocopying or otherwise, without the prior written permission of the publisher.

British Library Cataloguing in Publication Data

Tate, Robert Brian, *1921–*
  Pilgrimages to St. James of Compostella from the British Isles during the Middle Ages.
  1. Spain. Navarre. Pilgrimages to Santiago de Compostella. Christian history
  I. Title II. Series
  248.463094652

ISBN 0–85323–017–X

Photoset by Wilmaset, Birkenhead, Wirral
Printed in the
Printing Unit, University of Liverpool

PILGRIMAGES TO ST JAMES OF COMPOSTELLA FROM THE BRITISH ISLES DURING THE MIDDLE AGES*

The forename James in its various forms has always enjoyed a significant popularity in the British Isles. In modern times, as a Christian name, it falls well within the first four of saints' names. In terms of church dedications, the name of St James the Greater comes eighth in the list of preferences after Mary, All Saints, Peter, Michael, Andrew, John (the Baptist) and Nicholas. Not all the dedications are pre-Reformation, of course; James was regularly used as a dedication in the Northern Counties of England from the 1820s onwards.

The frequency of this saint's name can be attributed to several well-known circumstances. Of these the most important are that James was often referred to, with his twin James the Lesser, as brother to Christ, and that he was the first apostle to be martyred by Herod in Jerusalem as a result of his preaching to the Jews. Legend has it that his body and his head were conveyed by miraculous means to Spain where it was held that he had previously preached. The remains were disembarked at a small fishing village called El Padrón, on the northwest Atlantic coast of Galicia (Fig. 1). On the basis of these assumptions, the cult of St James was developed from the tenth century onwards. It took the form of a pilgrimage to his shrine, situated in a remote corner of Galicia called Compostella.[1] The church containing the shrine became, in its third version, a massive Romanesque cathedral under its first archbishop Diego Gelmírez (1060–1140); and in this same twelfth century became one of the three major pilgrimage centres of Europe.

* I would like to acknowledge my debt to Professor Derek Lomax who has written so widely on this topic, and particularly to Constance Mary Storrs' unpublished M.A. thesis for the University of London, *Jacobean Pilgrims from England from the Early Twelfth to the Late Fifteenth Century* (1964). I have not felt it appropriate to sketch out the ever-increasing bibliography on the subject. The following works are useful for consultation: J. G. Davies, *Pilgrimage Yesterday and Today. Why? Where? How?* (London: S. C. M. Press, 1988); R. A. Fletcher, *St James's Catapult* (Oxford: Clarendon Press, 1984); *La Quête du sacré. Saint Jacques de Compostelle* (Turnhout, Belgium: Brepols, 1985), a series of essays by experts introduced by Alphonse Dupront.

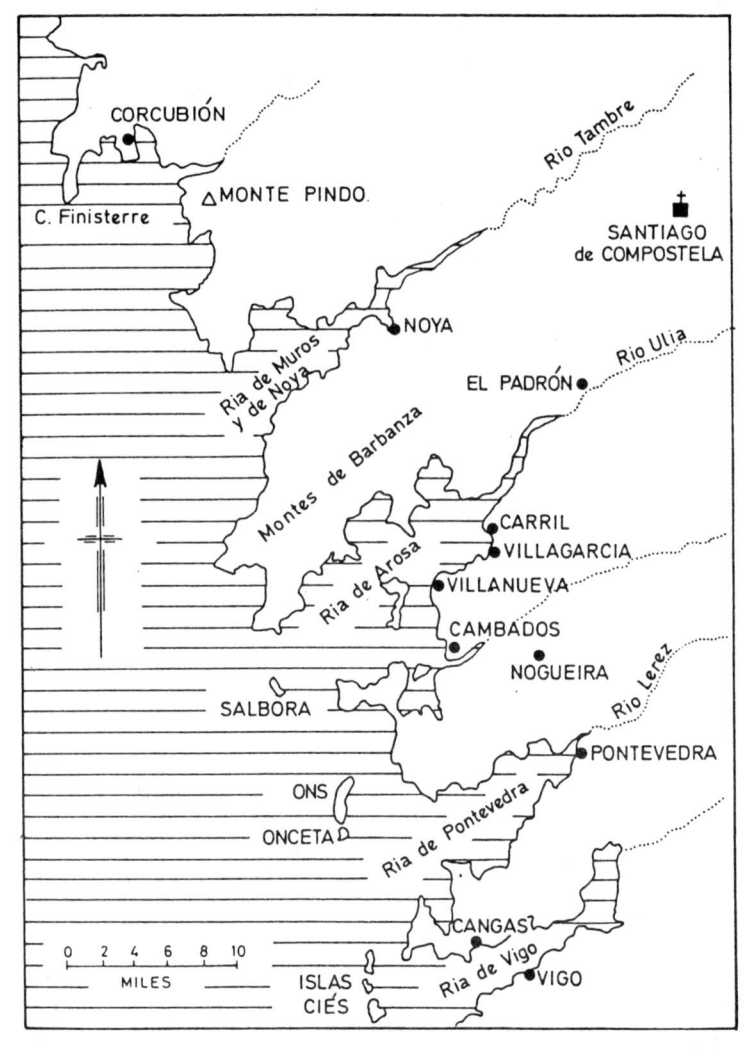

Fig. 1 Map of the Galician coast. From E. G. Bowen, *Britain and the Western Seaways* (London: Thames and Hudson, 1972), fig. 42.

A whole network of routes built up across Central Europe, flowing into four main routes across France (Fig. 2). These coalesced into two which crossed the Pyrenees at two passes, Roncevaux/Roncesvalles and Somport (*summum portum*). These in turn became one singular road at the river crossing point of Puente la Reina (Queen's Bridge), and along this route just south of the Cantabrian coastal range, the pilgrims straggled across the arid plains and the forests of Northern Spain. They then had to tackle the mountain ridges dividing León from Galicia, often thick with snow and ice, before descending slowly to the coastal plains and the shrine.

Why should this phenomenon become of interest at the present moment? One incontrovertible fact is that the number of visitors (they cannot all be called pilgrims) travelling the roads is steadily rising. All means of transport are being used: buses or campers which accompany the walkers, who do consecutive stretches every year; horses, although there are restrictive frontier regulations; bicycles—last year (1989) a penny-farthing bicycle was ridden from London to Spain for charity. Parish priests are grumbling at the uncontrolled numbers of young folk who want to sleep in their churches, barns, houses. It is still true that the main reason for journeying to Compostella is spiritual, but plenty of visitors walk or drive along the trail for other reasons: to experience the contrast of landscapes, to grasp a thousand years of history, to wonder at the architectural and cultural landmarks. Since the early 1980s the number of pilgrims has steadily tripled every year; the year before last (1988) more than four thousand came. This may well have increased a hundredfold with the Pope's visit in August 1989 for the Fourth Roman Catholic World Youth Day. And such crowds inevitably raise issues of conservation.

In 1987 the Council of Europe passed a new kind of conservation decree, urging member countries to preserve and signpost the traditional routes. In 1988 the Council called a European conference in Germany at which Great Britain was represented by Professor Lomax, who has just retired from the Chair of Spanish at Birmingham. At this conference in Bamberg it was discovered that, in contrast to other European countries, we in the British Isles had done very little coherent investigation of the pilgrimage to St James at Compostella. A number of volunteers, mainly associated with the recently founded Confraternity of Saint James, a non-sectarian

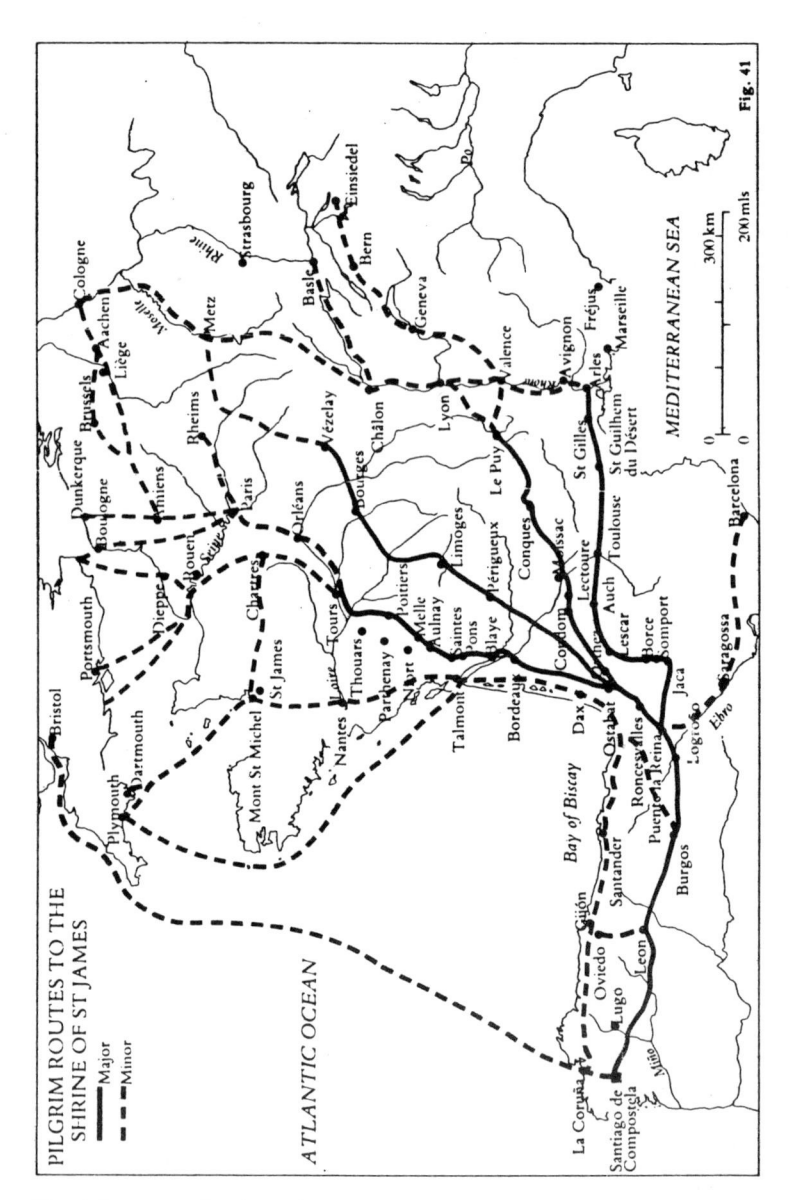

Fig. 2 Routes to Santiago de Compostella.

society based in London, promised we would do our best to assemble what data were available and to make preparations for assessing what remained to be done. My own personal experience derives from several trips along the routes over the past three decades, some with family and others with colleagues. The main results have been enshrined in a book of photographs with text published in 1987, the same year as the Council of Europe decree.[2] All these preceding events have led to an increased interest in the part played by pilgrims from the United Kingdom, and principally in the period of major traffic, the later Middle Ages.

I would like to survey the matter primarily as an historical phenomenon, under several headings:

1. General observations on the historical reasons for undertaking pilgrimage.
2. The geographical, political and commercial context of pilgrimage.
3. The freighting of pilgrims from the British Isles.
4. The points of embarcation along the coasts.
5. The transport used and the travelling conditions.
6. A sample of travellers' experiences.
7. Some visible and invisible remnants of the medieval cult in England.

1

The subject of pilgrimage cannot be studied in isolation from its social, historical, anthropological, devotional, liturgical and theological aspects. In a general conference on pilgrimage at Digby Stuart College in London in 1988, the topics ranged from pilgrimage rituals in Ayodya, India and the translation of ashes by British Hindus to the Ganges, to miracle and sacrifice discourse at Lourdes and other shrines. But, in brief, in terms of individual experience, pilgrimage can be said to consist in the pursuit of the spiritual dimension of life outside the daily routine, the search for physical and spiritual relief (both are profoundly linked), or the performance of an act of piety on behalf of oneself or someone else. Historically one can distinguish three main manifestations of early pilgrimage in European Christendom:

(a) *Exilic pilgrimage*. By this we understand that we human beings ultimately belong to another superior world; that the Christian suffers from permanent alienation hereunder. The Irish monks of the sixth and seventh centuries embraced this life as an ascetic exercise and established a tradition of permanent wandering:

> And three Scots [i.e. Irish] came to King Alfred in a boat without any oars from Ireland, whence they had stolen away, because they desired, for the love of God, to be in a state of pilgrimage, they cared not whither. The boat in which they had come was made of two and a half skins, and they took with them enough food for seven days, and then about the seventh day they came ashore in Cornwall. Thus they were named: Dubhslaine and Macbeathadh and Maelinmhain.[3]

Such wanderings by other pilgrims led to the foundations of the greater monasteries of Europe, like Bobbio in Italy, Rheinau in Germany and St Gallen in Switzerland.

(b) This practice diminished when the Benedictine rule was held to imply that stability was the mark of the monk. The pilgrimage then tended to be taken up, not only by religious, but by lay people from all strata of society, with a certain fixed goal in mind. The hardship of the voyage came to be considered as fitting into a proper and basic *penitential* category. By the thirteenth century the penitential pilgrimage was fully institutionalised and recognised as one of the legitimate forms of penance. From this practice sprang the granting of indulgences, a delicate subject to which I cannot do full justice here. These indulgences were given great impetus by Urban II in 1095 when he declared that crusaders who took up the cross would receive full remission of sins: crusaders were always considered as falling into the category of pilgrims.

(c) Lastly comes the *judicial* pilgrimage. A penitential pilgrimage could be transformed from an act of expiation into an instrument of punishment. It stood in part for the sentence of Cain, of the Wandering Jew, a condemned man with no fixed abode. Eventually sinners/heretics/criminals were sent to specific shrines. Here are two examples from the Registers of Bishop Hamo de Hethe of Rochester.[4] In the early fourteenth century Mabel de Boclonde had confessed adultery with Simon Heyroun. She was given the following punishment on 4 October 1326—to be beaten with rods six times around Woldham church, and as often around Rochester, Malling and Dartford markets: but in November the Bishop commuted this to pilgrimage to the shrine of St James at Compostella. Three years later, in another case, John Lawrence, clerk, was sentenced as one of the gang who had murdered Walter de Stapleden, Bishop of Exeter. He had struck the Bishop repeatedly on the head with the handle of a knife, but without drawing blood. He was to be beaten at the doors of all the churches in Rochester, clad only in breeches and barefoot, at the time when the crowd was greatest. As penance he was to take part in the next crusade, make a pilgrimage to Santiago and Notre Dame du Puy. He was to have mass said for the Bishop's soul for ten years and abstain from meat for life: he was not to shave for two years. Students of medieval Castilian literature will recall similar punishments meted out by the Virgin in Gonzalo de Berceo's *Milagros de nuestra señora*.

This shrine of St James first attracted attention outside Spain in the late ninth century. A martyrology of St Germain des Prés (*circa* 865 A.D.) notes for the first time that St James was buried 'in ultimis finibus' of Spain. A 'miraculous' location of the burial place had taken place, and the construction of a church begun. The first generous benefactor of one of the early churches was Alfonso III of León (866–910). He made several enquiries in France from the clergy of one of the most successful of saints' cults in France, St Martin of Tours, and in his letter he mentioned that miracles had occurred at the tomb. If this letter is authentic, it suggests that the cult was developing in mid-tenth century, and the phrase *patronus noster* began to occur in official documents. This choice of a patron saint to a royal house, and a martyr at the same time, is paralleled by similar acts throughout Europe. Wenceslas in Bohemia becomes a national saint in the tenth century. When France coalesced around the Capetian monarchy, St Martin and St Remy go into second place after St Denis, the first Bishop of Paris, murdered on Martyr's Hill, or Montmartre: Louis VI recognizes St Denis as patron saint in 1120. England shows little interest in these affairs: St George only becomes patron saint at the end of the fourteenth century. But none of these protecting saints becomes the focus of a major pilgrimage like that in Compostella, to which the whole of Western Christianity flocked in order to seek remission of sins, relief from suffering and spiritual rebirth. However, the honours done to the first apostle to be martyred were interpreted differently in the local context. For here the patron saint was not the humble evangelist, but the military figure on the charger, the Moorslayer, *Santiago Matamoros*, whose miraculous intervention in battle was to last from the Middle Ages in the Iberian Peninsula to the shores of the newly discovered continent of America. Shortly after the establishment of the shrine, distinguished visitors followed: the poet-bishop Gottschalk of Le Puy in 951, the Archbishop of Rheims in 961. An Arab poet wrote a panegyric on Almansur's expedition to Compostella in 997, and in it mentions pilgrims at the shrine. But the great opening surge in popularity begins after the Moorish threat had receded, after the conquest of Toledo in 1085: mass transit follows much later.

2

There are two obvious ways of travelling to Compostella: by boat and by foot or on horseback. Any pilgrim, rich or poor, had to make his mind up which dangers he could cope with best. On land he would be exposed to extremes of heat and cold, hunger, exhaustion, banditry and in the Later Middle Ages, endemic war. There were special dangers for women. In the Early Middle Ages an English missionary in Europe asked the Archbishop of Caterbury to prohibit matrons from going on pilgrimage across the sea: 'Few keep their virtue. There are many towns in Lombardy and Gaul where there is not a courtesan or a harlot but is of English stock'. (*Life of Boniface*).[5] Or again, a Christian captured by the Moslems was forced through starvation to kill his own daughter and eat her. Innocent II said this man was never to touch meat again, must fast through the week, never remarry and to go about unshod and in a woollen tunic. By sea, apart from the physical torments of what would be for the majority a first and only voyage by sea, there was also the weather in the Bay of Biscay, the wreckers on the shore, and pirates of every nationality. The length of the sea-journey varied. If one had a good tide and a favourable wind a ship could make the journey from, say, Poole in Dorset to La Coruña in five days. Roger Machado, ambassador of Henry VII to Castile and Portugal in 1488–89, made the journey from Falmouth to Laredo in six days in February and returned from Finisterre to Padstow, Cornwall in the same time. By land it could take upwards of six months there and back from Paris. However, one would have the inestimable advantage of recharging the spiritual batteries at a whole string of major shrines like Chartres, Poitiers, Tours, St Gilles, Toulouse etc. Andrew Boorde in the sixteenth century affirmed that the land journey through Spain was highly dangerous compared with the voyage to Rome. In his book, *The Introduction to Knowledge*, he describes how he met nine Englishmen and Scotsmen in France going to Santiago.[6] He tried to dissuade them, but they insisted and he reluctantly followed. They were starving when they reached Compostella, and only one, Boorde himself, survived the return journey. He adds that if he were on the King's council he would set in the stocks all those who set off without a licence. Furthermore, he would rather go five times to Rome than once from Orleans to Compostella.

The greatest number of pilgrims from the British Isles that we have information about tended to go by sea. Their pilots were simply following patterns of maritime movement that were well-established by the Phoenicians, the Romans and then the Vikings. (Figs. 3 & 4). The age-old link between the Atlantic and the Mediterranean was recast as a pilgrim route in May 1147 when one-hundred-and-sixty-four ships left Dartmouth carrying about thirteen thousand crusaders. Their intention was to join Louis VII in the Holy Land. En route, however, they celebrated Whitsunday in Compostella and captured Lisbon on 24 October. One of the pilgrim crusaders forgot his original aim and became the first bishop of Lisbon: Gilbert of Hastings. A perfect example of a Western seafarer turned pilgrim was St Godric of Finchale. He combined his merchandising in the North Sea and the Mediterranean with visits to major shrines, St Andrew, Rome, Jerusalem and St James. This last pilgrimage took place probably in the first decade of the twelfth century. Eventually, he settled near Durham in a hermitage, where he died in 1170.[7] The numbers of seaborne pilgrims eventually reached a climax in the early fifteenth century. An English pilgrim, William Wey from Eton, observed that when he was in the bay of La Coruña in 1458, he counted eighty-four ships from all the nations of the north. If we take a low average of sixty per ship, which was a common load, the total number would come to five thousand pilgrims disembarking in sequence over the various days.

It must be borne in mind that this particular traffic cannot be considered in isolation. The mass transit of pilgrims fluctuated inevitably according to the political and commercial plans of the

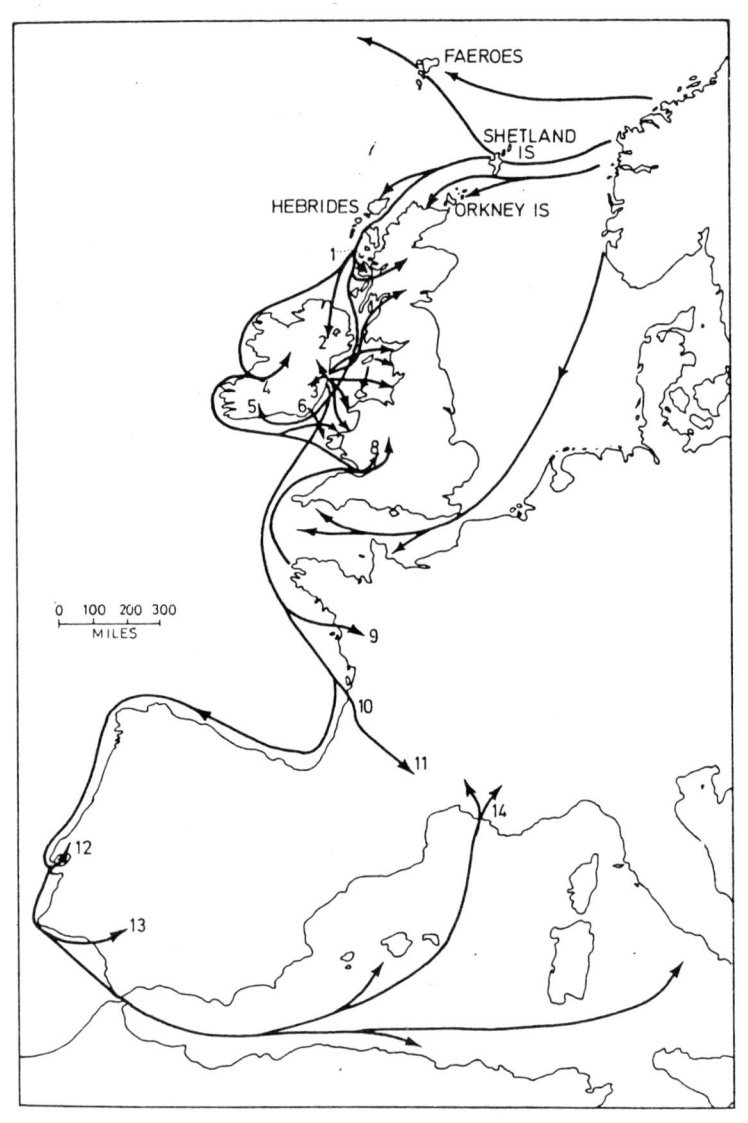

Fig. 3 Viking raids along Western Sea Routes. From Bowen, fig. 38.
1 Iona, 2 Armagh, 3 Dublin, 4 Limerick, 5 Cork, 6 Wexford, 7 St David's,
8 Archenfield, 9 Nantes, 10 Garonne, 11 Toulouse, 12 Lisbon, 13 Seville,
14 Rhône delta.

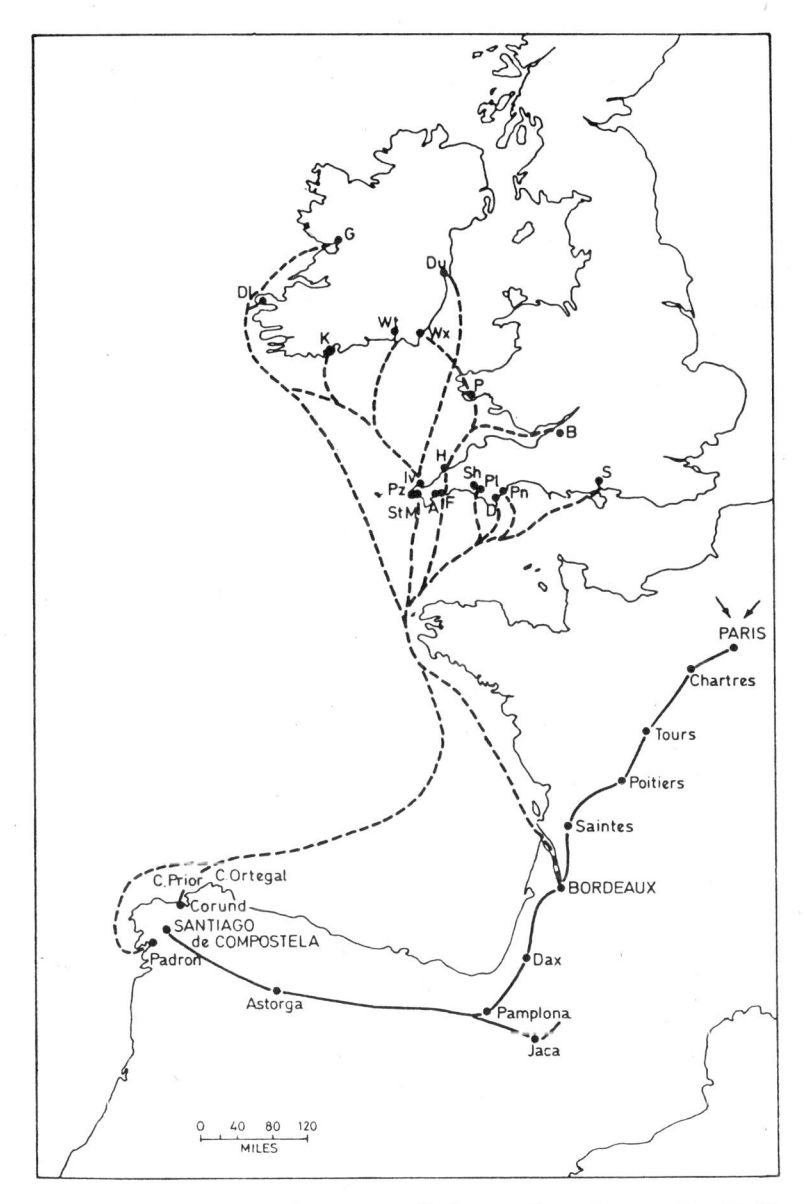

Fig. 4 Routes to Santiago de Compostella by sea. From Bowen, fig. 43. G Galway, Dl Dingle, K Kinsale, Wt Waterford, Wx Wexford, Du Dublin, P Pembroke, B Bristol, H Harlyn Bay, Iv St Ives, Pz Penzance, St M St Michaels Mount, A St Austell, F Fowey, Sh Saltash, Pl Plymouth, Pn Paignton, D Dartmouth, S Southampton.

three powers dominating the Atlantic coast—Castile, France and England; and the latter had one very large foot on the south side of the English Channel. The hostilities and pacts between these three nations alternated across the centuries, particularly from the thirteenth to the fifteenth centuries, according to the limits of English occupation of French soil. The classic Castilian-French alliance was never so close as to prevent the Castilians from dealing with the English. And there was scarcely a single English king who did not promise to make the journey to Santiago, from the times of Henry II to Edward I, II, III up to John of Gaunt, father of queens and kings. The same could be said of Philip of Valois. In fact none of them, with the single exception of John of Gaunt, ever got to Santiago. Both the French and English kings first promised then retracted, blaming each other for putting obstacles in their way. These promises did not always spring from exclusively spiritual reasons, as in the famous betrothal of Edward, Prince of Wales (Edward I) to Eleanor, sister of Alfonso the Wise of Castile in 1254.

One must also bear in mind that the most important French ports on the Atlantic were in English hands. Indeed, the Arabic geographer of the twelfth century, Idrisi, says that the English knew the Bay of Biscay so well that it was known as the English Sea. This of course facilitated the development of commercial routes from the English Channel to La Rochelle and above all to Bordeaux. The import of wine and the export of broadcloth made fortunes for the Merchant Venturers of Bristol and the Vintners Guild in London; and their ships were used for the carriage of pilgrims. The largest, like the Mary London of 320 tons took four hundred pilgrims to Santiago at the end of the fifteenth century. Merchants in the Channel ports, in Bordeaux, in the Basque provinces, Asturias and eventually Galicia, joined in the interchange of goods and pilgrims through the fourteenth and fifteenth centuries.[8]

3

Our main evidence for the movement of pilgrims by sea lies in the issue of shipping licences by the English crown. The earliest traceable so far is for 1235, but it seems an isolated case. English traffic acquires substance during the reign of Peter the Cruel of Castile (1350–1369) and increases during the civil and national wars that follow, despite the Schism and the excommunication of Castile, events which did not interrupt trade. The peak comes in 1434, a jubilee year when seventy-odd licences were issued. These official licences for the transport of pilgrims constitute the most reliable base for calculating the frequency of maritime movements, tonnage and the numbers of passengers. It goes without saying that the existence of an official permit does not mean that the voyage actually took place or that the number of pilgrims listed was actually heeded. In addition, many licences were valid for more than one voyage and sometimes the number of pilgrims was not fixed. On top of this the amount of unofficial traffic is incalculable. It is true that it was best to travel with papers: it might restrain pirates of one's own nationality. So, any general calculations must be hedged around with caution.

The number of pilgrims in any one ship varied between thirty and four hundred. This figure may not correspond to the entire capacity of the vessel, which might be carrying cloth or wine. If one bears all this in mind, and posits a figure of sixty per ship where no figure is given, then the total for the fourteenth century by sea will be five thousand pilgrims. For the first half of the fifteenth, peak point of the traffic, it is fourteen thousand pilgrims, nearly three times as much. The greatest quantity of traffic naturally falls in the jubilee years: 1428, 1434, 1445, 1451, 1456 etc. The business of transporting pilgrims *en masse* was not in the hands of the big operators. There were people of substance engaged, it is true, like the son of the Earl of Devon (Courtenay), or the Earl of Oxford (De Vere). From time to time, major merchants intervene, like Robert Sturmy, mayor of Bristol. He was the great pioneer of maritime enterprise of a later date, and member of the famous corporation of Merchant Venturers in Bristol, which still carries on today, though in a less aggressive form. In general terms, the greatest part of the pilgrim trade was in the hands of small shipowners, scattered down the southwest and southeast coasts of England in ports which today are mainly seaside resorts. We have as yet only sporadic evidence that ships carried both pilgrims and merchandise.[9] Official licences mostly mention carriage out and back in the same vessel, plus a week in Galicia. In the case of Venice, where the freighting of pilgrims was a massive undertaking, there was continual friction between the shippers and the authorities, who banned the mixing of cargoes. But the unofficial traffic in both types of freight went on, and what happened in Venice can hardly be exclusive.

4

The well-known Gough map of the fourteenth century gives some rough idea of the routes the pilgrims took to reach the main ports. But it is inevitably incomplete. Our task today is to try and establish some of these routes. These can be traced with difficulty through place names and dedications, or through documents like guild constitutions.[10] Of the ports where the pilgrims embarked, few have survived into the modern period as centres of commerce. On the east coast, the most northern is Newcastle upon Tyne: further south is Boston. Then there follows a string of small harbours from the Wash round to London, and along the Channel to the Severn estuary. If one divides this coastline into two areas, from Pembroke in Wales to Poole in Dorset; and from Lymington, Hants., to Newcastle, then it is the southwest sector which carries the most traffic. There are certain years when the east scores: 1390, 1451, 1473, 1484, but it is difficult to give any specific reason for this. If one then considers the total numbers of pilgrims from the licences (bearing in mind all the reservations given), then Bristol has the clear lead, with Dartmouth, Fowey and Poole following. On the east the totals are not so high. Southampton tops the list, then London, Winchelsea, Southwold, Cley and Cromer.[11]

In Ireland there were two important centres, one on the west and one on the east, Galway and Dublin. From these two ports the routes hugged the coast to the south and converged in the Bristol Channel to link up with the main traffic from the English Channel. This traffic then followed the protecting line of the Atlantic coast, although there is evidence that fast routes lay further out to sea. Most traffic went in convoy, as decrees of 1226 and later indicate. English, French and Castilian pirates roamed all these waters and did not often distinguish between friend and foe. One could be a pirate one year and a transporter of pilgrims the next, like Harry Pay of Poole. Poole itself was the object of pirate and political attacks. It was partly burnt by the French in 1377. Don Pero Niño, Count of Buelna, with three Castilian and two French galleys under the command of Charles de Savoisy managed to sack Poole in 1405 as a revenge for the burning of Norman towns and villages. Only the Castilians went ashore but they failed to fire the port: Harry Pay's brother was killed in the raid.

5

Pilgrims in mass transit travelled in very uncomfortable conditions. In the earlier centuries the ships were mainly of northern origin, cogs or hulks, single-masted and quarter-decked fore and aft. There was no physical distinction between poop and stern, merchant and warship. These ships are illustrated in the seals and arms of ports like Poole and Faversham (Fig. 5). In 1987 archaeologists, digging near the site of St James' church in Poole, unearthed the ribs of a boat some forty feet long and twelve to fifteen feet wide. These cogs were dominant between 1200 and 1400 in European trade. They had a horizontal keel not projecting below the bottom planks, and the hull form was wide and deep for maximum load. The Poole ship on the seal probably represented a fair size trading vessel of some hundred to hundred-and-twenty tons, this time with a vertical keel, length about sixty-six feet (excluding castles), and a beam of twenty feet. Hulks bulged outwards, and were rather like floating bananas. In the fifteenth century they were superseded by Mediterranean types like the caravel and the carrack. The central mast and square rig gave way to three masters with both square and lateen sails (Fig. 6).

There were naturally differences in the manner of carriage according to what you paid. William Wey, the Eton scholar, in the mid-fifteenth century recommends engaging a place in the highest part of the boat 'for the lawyst [stage] vnder, hyt ys ryght smolderyng hote and stynkyng'. On land 'be wel ware of dyuerse frutys, for they be not acordyng to yowre complexioun, and they gender a blody fluxe, and yf an Englyschman haue that sykenes hyt hys a maruel and scape hyt but he dye thereof'.[12] Those on mass transit had little to make life easy. The official licences stated clearly that on these ships there was only room for the lower orders: no nobles, knights, squires, clergy. They were to carry only sufficient money for the journey, and they were not to divulge state secrets. Pilgrims were given a space below of about six foot by two each and they slept with their heads towards the sides and their feet to the centre,

Fig. 5 Seals of Faversham and Poole. From F. W. Brooks, *The English Naval Forces* (London: A Brown & Sons, 1933) facing p. 80.

Fig. 6 An example of a carrack of 1511 with pilgrims aboard and a preacher on the sterncastle. Woodcut by Hans Burgkmair. From Roger Stalley, 'Sailing to Santiago from Northern Europe', *Future for our Past*, Council of Europe pamphlet 32 (1988), 10.

leaving a gangway in the middle. Cooking, if any, was done over a fire in the sand in the bilge. When the ship had put to sea, most accounts describe graphically the effects of sea-sickness, for which Malmsey wine was supposed to be a cure. In any case, the stench of an ill-lit and badly ventilated hold would, even without the ship's motion, be enough to turn the stomach. Everyone passed the time as best he could: some read, some sang and many played dice and cards. There were usually three religious services at daybreak, midday and evening. This last service was celebrated on the poop instead of beside the mainmast as in the morning. No consecrated elements were brought on board; so it was a 'dry' mass. The voyage, as has been said, could be as short as six days; but there were many holdups due to wind and tide, and the journey was often broken on the French Atlantic coast at La Rochelle, the Garonne estuary or at Bordeaux. The final port of call was La Coruña, or Corunna, or La Groyne as it appears in documents, near the old Roman *pharos*, marked on the famous Hereford map. There pilgrims could disembark in the massive sheltered harbour, rather like Poole. Little remains of the original waterfront, since it is now a good six hundred metres inland. The parish church of St James is still preserved in the old town, which has kept its ancient street names and patterns. From there it is a forty kilometre march to Compostella. Jean Froissart describes the arrival there in 1386 of John of Gaunt with his family and retinue. His fleet consisted of fifty-seven ships including the James (eighty tons) of Poole. I use Lord Berners' translation:

> The fyrst voyage they made, they wente to the chyrche and all theyr chyldren and made theyr prayers and offringe with grete giftes, and it was shewed me that the duke and the duches and theyr ii doughters, Phylyp and Katheryn were lodged in an abbay . . . other lordes, as syr John Holande and syr Thomas Moreaux and theyr wyves lodged in the towne and al other barons and knightes lodged abroad in the felde, in houses, and bowres of bowes, for there were ynowe in the countrey. They found there flesshe and strong wyne ynough, wherof the Englysshe archers dranke so moche that they were ofte tymes dronken, wherby they had the fevers, orelles in the mornyng theyr hedes were so evyl, that they coulde not helpe themselfe all the day after . . .[13]

It is during this period that one sees the maximum of interference by the English and French governments in the movement of pilgrims. At one point the English government tried to ban the transit of English and Gascon pilgrims to Santiago.

6

It would be impossible to list all the dignitaries, secular or ecclesiastical, who made the journey. Let me take three examples only. In the same year that the great ship Mary London left for Compostella in 1473, the most romantic of the Yorkist nobles took ship for the same purpose. Anthony Woodville, Earl Rivers, Baron Scales, commemorated this expedition on his arms, as did other families. He records the voyage as follows:

> I shipped from Southampton in the month of July the said year, and so sailed from thence till I came to the Spanish sea; there, lacking sight of all lands, the wind being good and the weather fair, then for a recreation and a passing of time I had delight and asked to read some good history. And among others there was in my company a worshipful gentleman named Louis de Bretailles which greatly delighted him in all virtuous and honest things, that said to me he hath there a book that he trusted I should like it right well, and brought it to me, which book I had never seen before, and is called the *Sayings or Dicts of the Philosophers*.[14]

This work has an ancient pedigree going back to the eleventh century; the Castilian version is known as the *Bocados de oro*, the Latin *Liber moralium philosophorum* and the French *Dits des philosophes*. This French version was translated by Rivers into English on his return and handed to Caxton in 1477. It was the first book ever printed in English. In the same year a royal presentation manuscript, now in Lambeth Palace Library, was made as a Christmas present for Edward IV on the same year.

A less well known pilgrim was Robert Langton, born in 1470 at Appleby in Westmoreland (Fig. 7). He was nephew to the famous Thomas Langton, Provost of Queen's College Oxford and Bishop of St David's, Salisbury and Winchester. His account of a pilgrimage to Compostella in the late fifteenth century is only to be found in a

Fig. 7 Brass of Robert Langton in Queen's College Chapel, Oxford. From Herbert W. Macklin, *The Brasses of England* (London: Methuen, 1907).

single pamphlet, printed in Fleet Street in 1522, at present in the cathedral library at Lincoln (Fig. 8). It is written in English and the frontispiece is a woodcut of a pilgrim and a friar beside a representation of a church and a castle. The inscription reads:

> The pilgrimage of M[aster] Robert Langton, clerke, to saynt James in Compostell and in other holy places of Christendome, with the name of every town and the space betwene them, as well by fraunce and spayne as the dutche way and other londes. And of the relykes and wondres in certayne townes and compendiously ordred as it appereth playnly in this present boke.

He also mentions 'Master Larkes book of the same', another pilgrimage account which must be lost. Langton follows the standard route in Spain. But at León he turns north to Oviedo, to San Salvador, across the Pajares pass. He then takes the coastal road to Betanzos and La Coruña where he slaves up 'a breakback hill' to Compostella. At Padrón he talks of St James' boat of stone in which the saint arrived in the little port: 'Also ye maste of stone under ye auter of the church wherein is the measure of his foot'. Langton then made a great circle down into Andalusia, back up through Valencia, into Italy and home through Germany. It was like an early version of the eighteenth-century grand tour.

Another pilgrim of note of the fifteenth century came from much humbler stock. He was called, according to a Galician document, Johannes Guadguar, which may be interpreted as John Goodyear. In 1456 he carried to the cathedral five alabaster panels in polychrome bas-relief, setting out the life of St James. They can be seen today high up on a wall of the Reliquary Chapel.[15]

There are five principal scenes:

1. Christ calls James the fisherman.
2. Christ sends the apostles out to preach.
3. James preaches (in Spain?).
4. James is martyred in Jerusalem.
5. The stone boat takes his body to Spain.

I know of no other example of a sculptured history of the life of St James. It must have been a special order, and may well come from Nottinghamshire, the source of many alabaster objects scattered throughout the continent.

⁋ The pylgrimage of M. Robert Langton clerke
to saynt James in Compostell. and in other holy
places of Crystendome, with the name of euery
towne and the space betwene them, as well by
fraunce & spayne as the dutche way and other
londes. And of the relykes and wōdres in certay
ne townes & places, compendiously ordred, as it
appereth playnly in this present boke.

Fig. 8 Frontispiece of *The Pilgrimage of Master Robert Langton, clerke*. From Lincoln Cathedral Library.

7

The remnants of the cult of St James are scattered across Ireland, Scotland, Wales and England. The list of artefacts and the documentary references are in the process of being collected. In the second category, bequests or instructions in wills are the most common; a few samples follow. John de Weston, brewer, offers his best silver girdle of scallops and forty shillings for a pilgrim to go on his behalf to Compostella after his death (1361). Margery Brown, relict of Thomas, offers ten marks for the same (1376). John de Holegh, hosier, elaborates further:

> To anyone making a pilgrimage to St James in Galis seven pounds, and if his executors be unable to find anyone to undertake such pilgrimage, then one half of the said legacies to be distributed among the poor, and the other to be devoted to the repair of roads within twenty miles of London. (1351)[16]

Objects fashioned in honour of St James are widely scattered. The earliest representation of the Saint in stone may well turn out to be a bas-relief panel in the porch of the parish church at Papplewick, Notts. This is a crude Romanesque seated figure with a tau staff in one hand and a shorter double staff in the other (perhaps broken) which could be dated earlier than mid-twelfth century. But many have disappeared, like the relic of a forearm of the apostle from the Abbey at Reading; like John Bawde's simple tabernacle once in the parish church at Woolpit, Suffolk;[17] or the few daubs of paint on the central arches of the nave of the parish church at Burgh-le-Marsh, Lincs.—all that is left of a great altar commemorating the escape from drowning of a group of pilgrims in the English Channel. The great statue of St James has vanished from the remains of the twelfth-century Benedictine Abbey of St James at Freiston, near Boston, Lincs. And In the same county all that marks the site of the fourteenth chapel of St James is the cemetery at East Allington. The old church of St James at Garlickhythe near the Thames in London has, however, been reborn twice. It was burnt in the Great Fire of London in 1666; it was then rebuilt by Wren and bombed in the Second World War. It has once more been restored, and last year (1988) the bracket clock, with its statue of St James on top and the scallop shell below, has been recreated to house the original works.

No-one that I know of has investigated the illuminated Books of

Hours in the British Library for images of the Saint. A number have connections with Spain. In a late fifteenth-century prayer book there is a seated St James as a pilgrim, with yellow cloak, hat and book in a landscape and a broad border of decorative staves and scallops; it also has portraits of Philip the Fair and Juana of Castile. Another vellum Book of Hours has a St James bareheaded with cloak, staff, scrip and book. The inscription states that it was presented to Isabella the Catholic by Francisco de Rojas, ambassador to Maximilian I when the marriage of Isabella's son Juan was being negotiated, as well as that of her daughter Juana.[18]

Conclusion

The phenomenon of mass-transit of pilgrims by sea from the British Isles is not an exclusive consequence of the fame of the Saint. Pilgrimage by sea depended on two factors: first, the increasing intensity of maritime coastal commerce from the thirteenth century onwards; second, the political and economic relations between England and Castile. Castile was dragged in as an ally in the major struggle between England and France over the Angevin inheritance. The opening of direct shipping routes from the Mediterranean to the north by the Genoese and the Castilians tied English trade to the European economy, and along those routes the pilgrims travelled. Politics and commerce fused in the marriage of Prince Edward and Eleanor of Castile. At that moment the English pilgrims who came by land flooded into Castile and provoked protest from the French. When Enrique de Trastamara murdered Pedro I of Castile, the Castilian pretender insisted that every English pilgrim should have the permission of the King of France. From then the majority took to the sea.

Post-Reformation history spent little time on pilgrimages. English writers followed no single line on this subject, but Thomas Cromwell followed Wyclif's views on relics. Most were destroyed, and pilgrimages were discouraged, unless they were 'internal' pilgrimages, like Bunyan's *Pilgrim's Progress*. The re-emergence of pilgrimage in the nineteenth century had little to do with Catholic Spain, and much more with the entrepreneurial spirit of Thomas Cook and Protestant England. He made his first organised sortie to the Holy Land in 1867 and was responsible for the visits of the future George V and Kaiser Wilhelm. The present dramatic increase in pilgrimage, not only to Compostella but elsewhere, has much to do with the dissatisfaction with aimless wandering, the desire for a sense of purpose and a chosen destination as a challenge. The emotions of escape, danger and romance cannot fail to emerge in Spain. At the centre of the experience is the journey, the space and the time for meditation, the conversations with others and above all with oneself and the angelic powers. The scenery may be the backdrop, but it is also part of the dialogue which stretches back to the great centuries of popular devotion.

NOTES

1 Various etymologies for the place name have been suggested. The most popular is the least likely, *campus stellae*, for it does not accord with the foundation legend. The Latin *compostum*, in diminutive form, a small burial place—suggestive of an earlier cemetery—is another possibility. Perhaps the most persuasive is *urbs composta*, that is, a new town laid out in the eleventh century after the last Moorish *razzias*.

2 Brian and Marcus Tate, *The Pilgrim Route to Santiago*, Photographs by Pablo Keller (Oxford: Phaidon Press, 1987).

3 *The Anglo-Saxon Chronicle*, trans. with an introduction by G. N. Garmonsway (London: Dent, 1965), 82.

4 *Registrum Hamonis Hethe* (diocese of Rochester, 1319–1352), ed. C. Johnson, Canterbury and York Series xlviii (Oxford: O.U.P., 1948), I, 201–02.

5 Ronald C. Finucane, *Miracles and Pilgrims. Popular Beliefs in Medieval England* (London: Dent, 1977), 40.

6 *The First Book of Introduction to Knowledge*, ed. F. J. Furnivall, Early English Texts Society Extra Series 10 (London, 1870), 205–06.

7 D. W. Lomax, 'The First English Pilgrims to Santiago de Compostella', *Studies in Medieval History presented to R. H. C. Davis*, ed. Henry Mayr-Harting and R. I. Moore (London and Ronceverte: Hambledon Press, 1985), 166, 170–72.

8 Wendy R. Childs, *Anglo-Castilian Trade in the Later Middle Ages* (Manchester: Manchester U.P., 1978).

9 Licences were given to Bristol merchants William Canning, Ellis Pell and Walter Derby in 1369 to take pilgrims to Galicia and 'bring thence merchandise and other victuals'. *CPR Edward III 1367–70*, 212, 226.

10 The guild constitutions in Lincoln, for instance, lay down the path southward for departing pilgrims to the Eleanor Cross originally set outside the Hospital of the Holy Innocents. At this point the guild members said farewell to the travellers. On their return, they would be met at the same point and accompanied back to the Cathedral for mass.

11 One of the ships leaving Plymouth in the jubilee year 1456 is called the Mayflower.
12 William Wey, *The Itineraries of William Wey . . . to Jerusalem A.D. 1458 and 1462: and to Saint James of Compostella A.D. 1456* (London: Roxburgh Club, 1857), 4, 6.
13 J. Froissart, *The Chronicle of Froissart*, trans. Sir John Bourchier, Lord Berners, with an introduction by W. P. Ker. Tudor Translations, 1st Series (London: D. Nutt, 1901–03), iv, 301.
14 George D. Painter, *William Caxton. A Quincentenary Biographer of England's First Printer* (London: Chatto and Windus, 1976), 87.
15 W. L. Hildburgh, 'A Datable English Alabaster Altarpiece at Santiago de Compostela', *Antiquaries Journal*, VI (1926), 304–07.
16 *Calendar of Wills proved and enrolled in the Court of Husting, London, 1258–1688*, ed. with an introduction by R. R. Sharpe (London: J. C. Francis, 1890), ii, 163, 221; i, 656.
17 *Wills and Inventories from the Registers of the Commissary of Bury St Edmund's and the Archdeacon of Sudbury*, ed. S. Tymms. Camden Society, O.S. 49 (London, 1850), 83.
18 British Library MS Section: Add. 17.280, f.344; Add. 18.851, f.412 and 437. Also Add. 48.985, f.84; Royal 20.D.VI, ff.17 and 20; Royal 2. A. XVIII, f.4; Add. 41.751, f.306; Add. 18.852, f.412 (with a portrait of the Infanta Juana of Castile on f.26); Eg. 1070, f.96.

THE FOURTH E. ALLISON PEERS LECTURER

Robert Brian Tate was educated at the Royal Belfast Academical Institution and at the Queen's University, Belfast, where he excelled as a student of the renowned Hispanist, Ignacio González Llubera. The war, and military service in the Far East, interrupted his studies, but he resumed them in 1946 and graduated with a First Class Honours degree in French and Spanish in 1948. He chose to write his Master's thesis on the work and ideas of Joan Margarit, Cardinal Bishop of Gerona, thus displaying at an early stage a profound interest in Catalan and Catalonia, which has endured to this day. In 1955 he completed his doctoral thesis, *The Influence of Italian Humanism on the Historiography of Castile and Aragón during the Fifteenth Century*, a study internationally recognized as a major contribution to our historical understanding of European Humanism in general and of Spanish culture and civilization in particular. Assistant Lecturer at Manchester University (1949–52), then Lecturer at the Queen's University, Belfast (1952–56), he moved to the University of Nottingham, where he was Reader and Head of Department in Spanish until he became, in 1958, the first holder of the Chair of Spanish at Nottingham, a position which he eminently occupied until his retirement in 1983. Professor Tate, an internationally acclaimed authority on the literature, history and ideology of the Middle Ages in Spain, has published numerous studies and critical editions in this field, including *Ensayos sobre la historiografía peninsular del siglo XV* (Madrid, 1970), *El cardenal Joan Margarit, vida i obra* (Barcelona, 1976), and editions of the works of Pérez de Guzmán, Fernando del Pulgar and Don Juan Manuel. He has recently completed a book, in collaboration with his son, Marcus, dealing with *The Pilgrim Route to Compostella* (Oxford, Phaidon, 1987). Professor Tate's outstanding contribution to Hispanic scholarship has been widely recognized internationally. He is a Corresponding Fellow of the Institut d'Estudis Catalans, Barcelona (1964), of the Real Academia de la Historia, Madrid (1974), and also of the Real Academia de Buenas Letras de Barcelona. In 1980 he was elected Fellow of the British Academy.

Previous Lectures in this Series

Reality Plain or Fancy? Some Reflections on Galdós' Concept of Realism
GEOFFREY W. RIBBANS

Geoffrey Ribbans, the first E. Allison Peers Lecturer, is a leading scholar of Galdós, who prior to his appointment to the William R. Kenan Jr Chair of Hispanic Studies at Brown University, Rhode Island, was – like Peers – Gilmour Professor of Spanish at Liverpool. Geoffrey Ribbans' lecture illuminates Galdós' concept of realism.

22 pp. Paper. £2.00/US$5.00   ISBN 0 85323 395 6

Gabriel García Márquez and the Invention of America
CARLOS FUENTES

Carlos Fuentes, the internationally known Mexican novelist and literary scholar, delivered the second E. Allison Peers Lecture at the University of Liverpool on 13 March 1987. His Lecture seeks to elucidate the nature of the modern Latin-American novel and the artistry of Gabriel García Márquez.

16 pp. Paper. £2.00/US$5.00   ISBN 0 85323 196 6

The Triple Janus Head of Romance Linguistics
YAKOV MALKIEL

Yakov Malkiel, formerly Professor of Romance Philology and Linguistics at the University of California, Berkeley, was the third E. Allison Peers Lecturer. Professor Malkiel is renowned worldwide for his research into Romance phonology, morphology, etymology, lexicography, sound symbolism, Latin prototypes, history of linguistics, and the theory of diachronic analysis. Although his lecture also deals briefly with the twentieth century, it focuses on the history of Romance philology from its inception in the late 1800s and traces its teaching from the nineteenth century, together with its development in various directions.

21 pp. Paper. £2.50/US$6.25   ISBN 0 85323 316 0